Productivity Techniques

How to Achieve More and Make Best Use of Your Time and Effort

Sarah Carter

All Rights Reserved worldwide. No part of this publication may be reproduced in any form or by any means, including scanning, photocopying, or otherwise without prior written permission of the copyright holder.

Copyright © 2020 Hook Heath Publishing

www.hookheathpublishing.com

About the Author – Sarah Carter

An ex-model that went on to become a successful freelance consultant in the financial services industry.

The books are based on the techniques used over the years in business working as a consultant.

It is deliberate the books are not too long, but sufficient to give you a background into the subject. After all, 'Brevity is the soul of wit', William Shakespeare.

Whether you are an author or have worked in financial services, I'd love to your story. My email is Sarah@hookheathpublishing.com

I have 4 books already published that you can find here under '**Recent Publications**'. They are all available free on Kindle Unlimited or in eBook or Paperback.

http://www.hookheathpublishing.com

Table of Contents

Productivity Techniques 1
About the Author – Sarah Carter 3
Table of Contents 4
Introduction 9
1.0 – Improving your Motivation 12
1.1 – Give yourself an Incentive................12
1.2 – Leave Yourself Notes........................14
1.3 – Set your Alarm Early.........................15
1.4 – Practice Positive Affirmations............16
1.5 – Have a plan and stick to it................16
1.6 – Start with a healthy Breakfast 17
1.7 – Stick to a morning Routine................17
1.8 – Include some exercise in your morning Routine 18
1.9 – Take One Step at a Time 18
1.10 – Keep Going 19
1.11 – Remember to Incentivise yourself ...19
1.12 – Your own Handwriting....................20
1.13 – Constantly evaluate your Performance 20

1.14 – Thin Slice your Tasks 21

1.15 – Focus on one task at a Time 22

1.16 – Use your support Network..............22

1.17 – Take a Break...................................23

1.18 – Consider what motivates You..........24

1.19 – Find some Music you Enjoy.............24

1.20 – Discover what works for You 25

2.0 Improve your Self-Discipline 26

2.1 – Have a Plan 27

2.2 – Stick to what you know Works 29

2.24 – Define Precise Goals.......................31

2.25 – Your Lifestyle should be designed to meet your Goals 32

2.26 – Plan Your Day in Advance 33

2.27 – Display Your Goals 34

2.28 – Explain to Yourself or Someone Else what you are Doing....................................34

2.29 – Congratulate Yourself.....................35

2.30 – Aim to do Better 35

2.31 – Stretch yourself to Achieve More 36

2.32 – Avoid having a Negative Mindset.....36

2.33 – Believe in Yourself..........................37

2.34 – Avoid Bad Habits...........................37

2.35 – Create a Daily Plan of Action 38

2.36 – What is my Why?..........................38

2.37 – Concentrate on Today 39

Chapter 3 – Time Management..................40

3.1 – Plan your Day 41

3.2 – Refine your Plan 42

3.3 – Use your Plan 42

3.4 – Build in some time to Relax...............43

Chapter 4 – Techniques for Daily Positive Thinking 44

4.1 – Don't take this Personally 45

4.2 – Look for the positive in any Situation .45

4.3 – Gather the evidence to support your positive thoughts......................................46

4.4 – Use Your Imagination 46

4.5 – Surround yourself with the right People 47

4.6 – Focus on the End Game....................47

4.7 – How you do Anything is How you do Everything 48

4.8 – Learn to Accept Yourself **48**

4.9 – Be Positive about other People **49**

4.10 – Be aware of what is around you **49**

4.11 – Reflect on your current thoughts and what is occupying your mind **50**

Chapter 5 – Achieving your Goals **51**

5.1   Focus on what you are want to Achieve **51**

5.2 – Break down your ultimate goal into smaller activities **52**

5.3 – Set a realistic timescale for each activity **52**

5.4 – Set New Goals when Achieved **53**

5.5 – Review Progress **53**

5.6 – Getting started is often Hard **53**

5.7 – Keep it Simple to at the Start **54**

5.8 – Set your Priorities **54**

5.9 – Keep your workload Realistic **55**

5.10 – Work with an Accountability Partner **55**

5.11 – Don't be surprised if something goes Wrong **56**

5.12 – Keep an eye out for people like minded people **56**

Introduction

Anyone can achieve more by learning how to set goals and achieve them in both their business and personal life. Even if you have set goals for yourself, it can still be difficult to accomplish everything you want to in your life. Most people find realising their goals a hard process.

We often put off doing what is required and struggle with having sufficient enthusiasm to achieve our goals. This can lead to, and ultimately fail to do what is required to deliver on our goals. This can lead to disappointment, leading us to become frustrated and a feeling of failure. By not delivering our goals can lead to losing confidence in ourselves making us feel inadequate in not moving forward with our lives.

Goal setting is a proven technique that helps us retain our motivation Setting goals can be a powerful tool that keeps us focused and keep focussed on the required task. Goals can act as the graphic and psychological prompt required to deliver what we need to do. Without setting the required goals, you are unlikely to achieve your desired outcomes.

Writing down your goals, reviewing them on a regular basis and 'ticking them off once achieved provides a huge lift to your self-confidence. This will inspire you to set new goals and deliver additional objectives to move your life forward. Achieving more goals leads to a better quality of life and attaining success that may have once have seemed beyond your expectations of what is possible in life.

Setting and achieving goals are techniques that you can learn and will only improve with practice. They help you become more control of your life.

Goals will help you become more organised and change your mindset. They make you more in control of your life for many reasons.

This book will help you achieve your goals with the following attributes –

- Enhanced motivation,
- Becoming more disciplined,
- Making better use of your time, and
- Improving your outlook on life.

1.0 – Improving your Motivation

Without sufficient motivation, you are unlikely complete the required actions to achieve your goals.

There are many ways to improve your motivation to achieve your goals. Below are some common examples of common techniques that can be used to increase motivation.

1.1 – Give yourself an Incentive

One technique is to use an incentive to complete the required task. For example, if you need to do some filing or raise some invoices, you might say to yourself once you complete this task you can watch a movie you want to see or go for a cycle ride.

The size of the reward should be appropriate to the size of the task. As another example, when I was studying to qualify as an accountant there was a sports car that had just been launched that

I really wanted to buy. But the deal with myself was once I passed the exams (which was 5 years work!) Then I could order my new car. This gave me the motivation I needed to complete the task.

1.2 – Leave Yourself Notes

There will be mornings when you don't feel like completing a task you need to do. This might be because you feel unwell or just in a bad mood.

It may also be because there is a task you just do not enjoy or have simply forgotten you need to do something tomorrow.

I write my notes on 'Post It' notes the night before and leave it somewhere I will see it in the morning. You can search the internet to find hundreds of motivational quotes or it may be a reminder of something you need to do in the morning, like make a phone call or send an email.

I was always trained to do the tasks you least want to do first in the morning to make for a productive day.

1.3 – Set your Alarm Early

By setting your alarm early in the morning, you effectively give yourself more time in the day to achieve your tasks and deliver your goals.

Imagine setting your alarm say an hour earlier 5 days a week, shows a positive motivational statement to yourself to achieve your goals.

It is also proven that too much sleep can affect your weight and adversely impact your health.

Likewise, hitting the snooze button on your alarm is starting the day with a negative motivational message to yourself. An extra 5 minutes in bed is going to do you far more harm than good and is a bad habit you should avoid.

1.4 – Practice Positive Affirmations

Talk to yourself and to encourage you can do what is required to get a task completed. This 'can do' attitude can the prompt you need to get the task completed rather than questioning if you have the ability by eliminating ay self-doubt.

1.5 – Have a plan and stick to it

Having a daily regular routine and sticking to it can make you far more productive. This is sometimes referred to as a 'well-trodden path'. The more often you have completed that routine the easier it gets and gives you the motivation and confidence to complete the task next time as you know you have the ability to get the job done. Sometimes you may have to deviate from your routine but where possible stick to what you know works best.

This is why sometimes it is a good idea to have a checklist for a task to make sure everything is done correctly; nothing is forgotten and in the delivered in the right order.

1.6 – Start with a healthy Breakfast

Positive affirmations and starting the day with a healthy breakfast helps make for a productive day. Eating the right food in the morning gives you the energy to achieve your tasks and goals.

It's a bad move to avoid breakfast, even if you feel you don't have enough time. Make sure breakfast is part of your daily routine to achieve the most from each day.

1.7 – Stick to a morning Routine

Develop a morning routine to get you motivated to have a successful day. The more you practice the routine, the easier it will become and you will complete many activities without having any doubt on your ability to get the tasks done. You know how to perform each task with confidence and you know what you the task you have to do next.

Deviations from your routine will make it more difficult to have a productive day as the different routine will feel less familiar. The opposite is also true as doing the same things in the same order will help you feel more confident you are going to have a productive day.

1.8 – Include some exercise in your morning Routine

Exercise in the morning can help motivate you to help you get through the day. Including a walk, cycle, run or a trip to the gym can help increase your blood circulation and stop you feeling tired

1.9 – Take One Step at a Time

Focus your mind on one thing at a time. If you try to consider everything at once, you will feel distracted and unproductive. Give the task you are working on the Concentrate on the task you are working on at the moment your full attention until it is complete. This is the best way to achieve more and not waste your effort.

1.10 – Keep Going

Sometimes that hardest part pf any task is to get started, particularly with a task you do not really joy, know it needs to be done. There is no 'on/off' switch.so once you get started it is important to keep going forward. Sometimes you just need to force yourself to keep going. Keep going until the task is complete and you have achieved what you set out to do. There is no time like the present to get the job done and you don't want to end up with lots of incomplete tasks.

1.11 – Remember to Incentivise yourself

In difficult situations, setting yourself an appropriate reward can help with your motivation to complete a task. This will help you keep going and get the job done.

1.12 – Your own Handwriting

Your own handwriting is unique and the best way to remember something is a not in your own handwriting. In contrast, a note written by someone else is the hardest to retain in your mind. A typed message is somewhere between the two. Therefore, if you want to motivate yourself or remember something important write it down in your own handwriting.

1.13 – Constantly evaluate your Performance

Sometimes we are so busy thinking about what we need to get done that we forget about how much we have actually achieved. Keeping a diary of what you have done each day can be a useful way to periodically review what you have done since your last review. Make time to review what you have achieved, say weekly or monthly so you can reflect on how things have gone. Did you achieve what you set out to do in the period?

Could you have done anything better? Is there anything you have discovered that will be useful for future reference? Focus on the positives as well as the negatives, so you learn how to achieve more next time.

1.14 – Thin Slice your Tasks

Sometimes it is easy to feel discouraged It is extremely easy to de-motivate yourself where a task feels too big and unachievable. By breaking down one large task into multiple smaller sub tasks, sometimes known as 'thin slicing', you can make a task feel more achievable and reduce the risk of feeling overwhelmed by the task in question. This can also be used to split a task across multiple people and maybe get the task completed quicker.

1.15 – Focus on one task at a Time

Sometimes you may feel the need to work on many activities at the same time.to clear your workload. It may appear a good idea, but the reality demonstrates it is not an efficient way of working. Each task needs your undivided attention, so by constantly changing between tasks wastes a lot of time and the overall time required to get all the tasks done will be longer.

1.16 – Use your support Network

Always consider your network of friends and family as a great source of motivation. However, choose people carefully as negative or unsupportive individuals can have the opposite effect. People will surprise you (in a good or bad way) and sometimes you can be too close to the problem or over think the solution.

1.17 – Take a Break

In hard times, it is all too easy to feel demotivated and everything seems to appear too difficult. If this happens (and it will!) take a step back and consider applying some of the other motivational techniques in this book. Everyone is different but you will get to learn what works best for you. Often just trying something slightly different. For example, I like to build a short cycle ride into my daily routine. But sometimes I find just changing my route can have a positive effect on my motivation.

1.18 – Consider what motivates You

If feel you lack energy or enthusiasm for the task in hand, some people like to ask themselves 'what is my why?' It might be you are saving for a holiday or a new car. It might be to provide for your family. Again, everyone is different and will have their own reasons for their own motivation.

Reflecting on why you are doing a particular task may be just the inventive you need to push forward and get the job done.

1.19 – Find some Music you Enjoy

I often find listening to music can help give me more positive outlook and improve my motivation and energy levels. There is often a link between music and positive events that have happened in your past. For example, you may remember going to a concert or being on a memorable holiday when you first heard that song.

1.20 – Discover what works for You

Not all the suggestions in this book will work for everyone. Try different things and find what motivates you.

Some of the ideas in this book sound very similar or apply common techniques. As stated earlier, repetition and familiarity are no bad thing and sometimes just by explaining things in a slightly different way can help more people grasp the concepts and become more motivated.

2.0 Improve your Self-Discipline

Being self-disciplined is a great way to improve your productivity and achieve more success.

Sometimes it can be difficult to stay focussed and deviate from the planned activity. There can be temptations to deviate from what you know you should be doing to achieve your goals.

Self-discipline is a technique to keep you on track and trigger warning signs if you are going in the wrong direction to complete your tasks. It will help you realise when you are taking too much on. Below are some common techniques to develop that self-discipline and keep you moving in the right direction.

2.1 – Have a Plan

"Failing to Plan is Planning to Fail"
Unknown

The quote first appeared in articles in the late 1970s. However, the sentiment behind the quote is just as relevant today.

Having a planned routine to complete a task or tasks takes time to develop and should be periodically reviewed to see if there is scope to improvement in the plan, particularly when things have gone wrong. The plan may have been suitable when originally developed, but circumstances change over time.

Building the plan into your routine will help make sure the tasks are completed correctly and in the right order. This reduces the scope for errors and ensures you do not forget any tasks.

The plan will also have other benefits like giving you a future reference for how long a task should take and can help if you are looking to delegate the task to someone with less experience.

The plan could be as simple as a checklist, e.g. you might check cupboards for what you need to buy before you go shopping for groceries in a supermarket. This can help you avoid forgetting an item and reduce the likelihood of impulse buying if you are trying to keep to a limited budget.

Progress should be periodically reviewed against the plan to make sure you are on course to complete the task on time and within budget. If it emerges your progress is behind where the plan says you should be, you may need to consider reprioritising your workload. However, it is important to understand why you are behind where you should be on the plan. This could be something personal like sickness or something technical like a computer failure.

2.2 – Stick to what you know Works

Wherever possible, try to avoid deviating from your plan. Again, the repetition and knowing a certain approach works well gives you one less thing to worry about.

For example, if you know a certain supplier is most likely to have an item in stock or maybe at the best price or quality, you will have more confidence of being able to complete the task of purchasing the item. Maybe you know to best approach is to check the item is in stock before taking time out of your day for a wasted journey.

It maybe that you know completing two tasks at the same time is the most effective approach. For example, if you are travelling to a business meeting, you might want to schedule multiple meetings for the same day in that location. However, your experience will tell you how long to takes to get to that destination or how long that meeting might last.

Again, an agenda for the meeting is a good way to plan ahead of what you would like to discuss so there are no surprises for any party involved in the meeting.

Maybe you allocate a set amount of time for the meeting and each item on the agenda. This is also useful if say someone is only required for part of the meeting, so they don't need to attend for the whole time.

If you find something occurs that means deviating from your routine, try to get back to your normal work pattern as quickly as possible.

Invariably sometimes you might need to make priority decisions to establish which activity is most important.

2.24 – Define Precise Goals

Setting precise goals is an important step in achieving your desired outcomes. Without goals you will not know whether you are heading in the right direction. Set the goals before you start working on any activity so that you have a clear idea of what you are trying to achieve, how to get there and the benefits of achieving those goals. This will also help with your motivation to keep going as you will know why you need to complete the activity. This will help you keep going when times are tough as you will have a clear understanding of why it is important to complete the activity and the benefits of doing so.

2.25 – Your Lifestyle should be designed to meet your Goals

By having a clear understanding of what you want to achieve will help motivate you to work on the activities to complete your goals. When you have it clear in your mind what you want to achieve and you have a set of goals, which are the stepping stones to get you there, you can start to organise your life to best help you achieve those goals. This could be as simple as setting yourself a daily routine, as discussed earlier in this book.

2.26 – Plan Your Day in Advance

Organise your day in advance so that you know what you plan to achieve that day and have everything to hand to complete those activities. This may only take a few minutes but it stops you losing momentum during the day when you have to stop and look for something essential. Some people like to do this first thing in the morning whereas others prefer to do it at the end of the previous day. Planning ahead may also include deciding which order to complete tasks and which tasks to group together. It is often recommended to complete the task you find the hardest or least enjoy doing first. It is too easy to complete the more enjoyable tasks first but this is just putting off the harder tasks until later in the day.

2.27 – Display Your Goals

Position your goals somewhere prominent so that you will see them on a regular basis. This could be on a wall (e.g. a corkboard or whiteboard) or in a simple picture frame on your desk. The repetition of looking at your goals will help keep you motivated and remind you why you are going to the effort to complete these goals. This is a quick and effective way to keep you un track to achieve your goals.

2.28 – Explain to Yourself or Someone Else what you are Doing

It is one thing to know what you need to do to complete an activity, but far better if you can explain what and why you are doing it to yourself or someone else. Talking about what you are doing is another way to gain clarity and the confidence you are heading in the right direction or approaching an activity in the best way. Talking gives you that awareness.

2.29 – Congratulate Yourself

When you feel disappointed you have not achieved everything you wanted to get done, remind yourself of what you have achieved, however large or small. It is too easy to be negative and criticise yourself if you have not achieved everything you wanted to do. However, it is far more productive to be positive and congratulate yourself on what you have achieved. This is a far greater motivator to keep going throughout the day.

2.30 – Aim to do Better

Challenge yourself to achieve more than you did in the past. This will encourage you to be more productive and look for better ways to get the job done quicker. Ask yourself if that task is still necessary or over complicated as sometimes the reason for the task may no longer be valid and you are clear in your mind why a particular task is necessary.

2.31 – Stretch yourself to Achieve More

Always strive to push yourself to achieve more by taking on new and more difficult tasks. In doing so, you will keep yourself motivated with the constant challenge to improve yourself rather than just completing the same tasks again and again.

Sometimes a bit of competition from with others can also help your motivation and keep you moving forward.

2.32 – Avoid having a Negative Mindset

In order to set effective goals, you need to be in a positive frame of mind. Any negative thoughts will adversely affect your ability to make the right decisions. You need to practice clearing your mind of negative thoughts and look for the positive in any situation.

2.33 – Believe in Yourself

Make a deal with yourself to do whatever it takes to complete your tasks and achieve your goals. Tell yourself you can achieve what is required and avoid any thought you are no up to the job in hand. This is not an easy thing to do but like many suggestions in this book, the more your practice and build them into your routine the task will become easier.

2.34 – Avoid Bad Habits

To achieve your goals, you need to work on avoiding any bad habits. Instinctively most people know if they have any particular bad habits. Make a list of them and work on removing them from you daily life. By doing this you will become a better person to focus on achieving your goals. Make a note to review the list periodically to see how you are doing and add any new bad habits to the list.

2.35 – Create a Daily Plan of Action

Create a daily action plan and strive to achieve all the actions each day. I personally like to run two action plans, one for personal activities and one for business activities. Before adding something to your action plan, consider is this taking me towards my goals. If actions seem too large, consider breaking them down into smaller sub actions that may feel more manageable to achieve. As ever, keep the contents of this action plan under constant review as the required actions will change over time.

2.36 – What is my Why?

When you feel you are lacking motivation, take a few minutes out to consider why you are completing this task and how it fits into meeting your wider goals. Another option is to write down your goals as the first activity every morning. This simple routine will help you remember why you are completing these tasks to meet your goals.

2.37 – Concentrate on Today

Focus on the present day and where you are now. This is where your attention should be with the objective of completing the tasks you need to complete today.

As said before it is important to constantly remind yourself of your goals, but you will find it hard to achieve you goals if your priority is not the tasks you need to complete today.

Likewise, spending a lot of time thinking about the past is unlikely to be productive. You cannot change what happened in the past but you can learn from it. For example, learn from your mistakes so that you do not repeat them and remind yourself if you have completed a task before that you know you have the ability to complete that task.

Chapter 3 – Time Management

Time management is a series of techniques to increase effectiveness and productivity. The process involves making detailed plans and careful monitoring of time spent on each activity.

The process involves balancing a person's time between multiple types of activity, including work, leisure time, family, interests being aware that all these activities are important but each of us only has a limited amount of time. Hence there is a need to use the time do have wisely.

Various techniques are used to assist with time management breaking down goals into projects and tasks, each with their own deliver date.

The original concept of time management was conceived to focus on business related tasks and activities. However, the application of the techniques has now branched into personal activities. A time management system is a structured approach to make sure all activities are completed on time and in the correct order. The system will consider, effectiveness, priorities and ultimately achieving goals.

3.1 – Plan your Day

Start your day by considering what tasks you need to complete today. Use your best judgement to allocate time to each task. Then as each task is completed, make a note of how long the task actually took to complete. It is useful to make notes of why a task to more or less time to complete for future reference. If these are repetitive tasks your estimate for time will improve as you learn more about how long it actually took and why. So, the concept is you learn from the experience of completing the task so that you are more prepared next time you need to complete the task.

3.2 – Refine your Plan

Consider the best order to tackle the tasks you need to complete in the day. This may involve grouping similar tasks together, tackling higher priority or more complex tasks first before moving onto lower priority tasks.

3.3 – Use your Plan

Your plan is a living working document. There is no point having a plan unless you actually use it to guide you through your day. In fact, unless you actually use the plan, it is actually time wasted in your day.

Sometimes you may need to deviate from you plan. In this situation, deal with the unexpected activity and get back to your original plan as quickly as possible.

3.4 – Build in some time to Relax

Sometimes you may think you are too busy to take a break. This tends to be counterproductive over a period of time, so build in some downtime. This does not need to be a time-consuming process, but a coffee or lunch or colleague or friend might just help you recharge a little. It also breaks up your day and might give you something to look forward to as well as some well-deserved rest. Other might like to read a book or go for a run or cycle.

Chapter 4 – Techniques for Daily Positive Thinking

Positive thinking is very constructive whereas negative thoughts are very destructive. Everybody We all have fears and worries – but you need learn to process and eliminate negative thoughts.

Below are some techniques to encourage positive thoughts, even in difficult times. This will help you remain focussed and confident in completing the task and take you closer to achieving what you desire.

4.1 – Don't take this Personally

Most people's actions are a reflection on them rather than something you have done. Constantly remind yourself that you are not responsible for other people's actions.

4.2 – Look for the positive in any Situation

Avoid spending your life reflecting on negative thoughts as this will not take you towards achieving your goals. Don't complain, look for the positives and move on. It is much better to focus on the positives and what is good about your life.

4.3 – Gather the evidence to support your positive thoughts

Make a small list of positive thoughts and then focus of looking for examples or evidence to demonstrate your reasons to be positive in any situation.

This simple technique has many benefits but in particular will help you feel better about the situation and change the way you approach any issues in the future.

4.4 – Use Your Imagination

Imagine what it will feel like to achieve your goals as a positive way to focus on competing the tasks to get you to you ultimate desired outcome. Subconsciously this will place another reminder in your mind of what you are trying to achieve.

4.5 – Surround yourself with the right People

The people you spend most time with will have a significant impact on your mindset and your ability to achieve your goals. If the people around you are having a negative influence, this will be destructive to your own success. Ideally try and surround yourself with people who have achieved the kind of success you are looking for in your goals. You should not be the smartest of most successful person in your network, as this will not drive you to achieve more.

4.6 – Focus on the End Game

Focus on achieving your long-term goals. It is fine to reward yourself for completing individual activities, but keep the reward proportionate to the size and effort of the task.

4.7 – How you do Anything is How you do Everything

This is a quote from one of my mentors that has always stuck in my mind. The principle is that you should strive to do everything to the best of your ability and consistent with your highest standards of ethics and quality. Once you let your standards deviate from this rule, there is always a risk you will do the same in other parts of your life.

4.8 – Learn to Accept Yourself

Find Acceptance inn yourself and avoid any negative thoughts caused by comparing yourself with other people. Instead, focus on being 'the best possible you'

4.9 – Be Positive about other People

Look for the good in other people and over time you will find people look for the good in you. Likewise, if you are always looking to criticise other people you will receive a negative reaction from others. Treat others how you would expect them to treat you.

4.10 – Be aware of what is around you

Observe your surroundings in your daily life. This helps stimulate your mind and awareness. This routine of observing detail will become automatic and extremely useful in your future activities.

4.11 – Reflect on your current thoughts and what is occupying your mind

Be aware of what you are thinking about. Maybe keep a diary of what you are thinking about and then decide whether the thoughts are important and helpful. As with negative thoughts, consider if they are taking you towards your goals, otherwise lean not to dwell on them and pay more attention what is good and positive in your mind.

4.12 – Be alert and Focus on the Present

Maximise your focus all your attention on your current activity in hand. Thinking about other activities is just a distraction from the task in hand and are likely to lead to extended timescales to complete an activity on time.

Chapter 5 – Achieving your Goals

In order to achieve your goals, they need to be realistic. There is nothing wrong with dreams and ambition, but in this chapter, we will show you how set the right goals for you.

5.1   Focus on what you are want to Achieve

Unless you are clear what you are trying to achieve and why that is important to you, it will be difficult to remain focussed on achieving your goals.

5.2 – Break down your ultimate goal into smaller activities

Break your main goals down into smaller activities that will individually appear more achievable. There may be multiple layers of these sub activities. Once you have achieved all the sub activities

5.3 – Set a realistic timescale for each activity

Consider each individual activity and allocate a reasonable timescale to complete the task to the standard you expect. However, take care not to set your timescales too short and too long.

By considering the timescale for each activity, you can derive a realistic timescale for the entire goal.

5.4 – Set New Goals when Achieved

Setting and Achieving Goals is not a one-off process. When your Goal has been achieved, remember to reward yourself, but start working on setting new goals straight away to build on your success.

5.5 – Review Progress

Allocate time to review your process on activities against your plan on a regular basis. The appropriate frequency of such reviews will depend on the size of the activities and the criticality of meeting deadlines, particularly if you are behind schedule.

5.6 – Getting started is often Hard

When you have identified the goals you want to achieve, take the time to follow the relevant steps in this book, like creating a plan, identifying the activities required and breaking them down into smaller activities.

5.7 – Keep it Simple to at the Start

Start with some easier goals to start with in the early days while you get into the routine of setting and achieving goals. Then you will feel more confident to gradually increase the size and complexity of your goals.

5.8 – Set your Priorities

Work out what is most important in your life to achieve. The best way to do this is to make a list of all the things you would like to achieve and sort them into order with the highest priority items first. Once you have your highest priority goals, do not discard the list as it will become a working document. The next time you want to set new goals to work, you can review this list and possibly reprioritise the goals, as your priorities will change over time. At this point you might find some goals are not required anymore and can be removed, or new ones need adding to the list.

5.9 – Keep your workload Realistic

Avoid the temptation to try and do too much. This is not sustainable for any period of time and you will just become frustrated when you miss your deadlines. Instead, look again at your priorities and work out which activities are actually necessary right now. Anything that is not essential should be rescheduled to a later date when you have more time.

5.10 – Work with an Accountability Partner

An accountability partner is someone who will periodically review your progress and make sure you stay on track to achieve your goals. Sometimes just knowing you soon have a catch up with your accountability partner is the nudge you need to complete a task or at least be able to explain why you are behind schedule.

5.11 – Don't be surprised if something goes Wrong

It is inevitable that, from time to time, this will not go as planned or circumstances change that were unexpected. This could be you have made a mistake or somebody else. Either way, you need to learn to put such events behind you, take any correcting actions and get back on schedule as quickly as possible. The only thing you can do is to assess the likelihood of it happening again and the consider the appropriate actions to avoid a reoccurrence of such an event in the future.

5.12 – Keep an eye out for people like minded people

One of my Mentors always says 'Your Network is your Net Worth'. Listen to what people are saying and of course it costs nothing to be polite. You will be surprised how interesting people come into your life.

www.ingramcontent.com/pod-product-compliance
Lightning Source LLC
Chambersburg PA
CBHW030510220526
45464CB00006B/2738